Bank failure: Evidence from the Colombian financial crisis[1]

Jose E. Gomez-Gonzalez[2]
Cornell University and Banco de la República

Nicholas M. Kiefer[3]
Cornell University and US Department of the Treasury,
Office of the Comptroller of the Currency

OCC Economics Working Paper 2007-2

March 15, 2007

[1]Disclaimer: The views herein are those of the authors and do not necessarily represent the views of the Banco de la Republica or the Office of the Comptroller of the Currency. Acknowledgement: We thank seminar participants at Banco de la Republica and the OCC for helpful comments.
[2]jeg44@cornell.edu. 445 Uris Hall, Department of Economics, Cornell University, Ithaca, NY 14850, USA.
[3]nmk1@cornell.edu. 490 Uris Hall, Department of Economics and Department of Statistical Science, Cornell University, Ithaca, NY 14850, USA.

Abstract

Bank-specific determinants of bank failure during the financial crisis in Colombia are identified and studied using duration analysis. The process of failure of banks and related financial institutions during that period can be explained by differences in financial health and prudence across institutions. The capitalization ratio is the most significant indicator explaining bank failure. Increases in this ratio lead to a reduction in the hazard rate of failure at any given moment in time. This ratio exhibits a non-linear component. At lower levels of capitalization small differences in capitalization are associated with larger differences in failure rates. Our results thus provide empirical support for existing regulatory practice. Other important variables explaining bank failure dynamics are the bank's size and profitability.

JEL Classification: C41; E4; E58; G21; G23; G38

Keywords: Financial institutions, bankruptcy, liquidation, capitalization, supervision, duration hazard function.

1 Introduction

During the late 1990s and early 2000s, Colombia's financial system experienced a period of financial stress, characterized by the failure of many banks and other financial institutions, as well as by the severe deterioration of the whole system's financial health. The capitalization ratio of the system fell dramatically, as did profitability and liquidity. As a consequence of the crisis, the number of institutions[1], 110 in June 1998, dropped to only 57 in December 2001, after failures, mergers and acquisitions. Total assets of the financial system experienced a real contraction of more than 20 percent during the same period, making that episode of financial stress the deepest financial crisis experienced by the country in the last century.

The literature on the financial crisis of Colombia has concentrated on explaining its causes and consequences. See Arias et al (1999), Arbeláez et al. (2003), Carrasquilla and Zárate (2002), Parra and Salazar (2000), Uribe and Vargas (2002), Urrutia (1999) and Villar et al (2005). There have been no micro-level studies of the role of specific financial variables in determining failure and time to failure of banks. This paper uses duration models to characterize the failure rates of financial institutions in Colombia and to identify key financial variables associated with these failure rates. Duration models use hazard functions rather than densities to specify the distribution of observables (and thus the likelihood function). For the method, see Kiefer (1988) and Lancaster (1990). Although early economic applications of hazard functions or duration analysis were in labor economics, they have been applied to bank failures. Lane et al (1986), Weelock and Wilson (1995), and Whalen (1991), use duration models to explain bank failure in the United States. Other studies have used duration models to explain time to failure after particular episodes of financial stress in under-developed countries. For example, Gonzalez-Hermosillo et al (1996) use them to explain bank failure after the Mexican crisis of 1994, and Carree (2003) does a hazard rate analysis of Russian commercial banks in the period 1994-1997.

There are theoretical as well as practical reasons to consider that the capitalization ratio plays a special role for financial institutions. The literature on capital crunch shows that, under capital regulations, this ratio is important for financial

---

[1]The financial system here includes commercial banks, financial companies, and financial companies specialized in commercial leasing. Financial cooperatives and special public financial institutions are not included here.

institutions when they are making decisions on portfolio composition. See Peek and Rosengren (1995), Estrella et al (2000), and Van den Heuvel (2004). In the practical world, following the Basel accord (Basel Committee on Banking Supervision, 2004), financial institutions and supervisors now follow closely the capital ratio of the institutions they regulate and impose minimum requirements. Thus, capitalization plays a special role for financial institutions in determining their overall financial health and thus the degree of trouble that they might experience in episodes of financial stress. We focus on the capitalization variable and identify a nonlinear effect. As might be expected, increasing the capitalization ratio decreases the probability of default at a decreasing rate. Although capitalization is sometimes one of several significant variables, previous studies have not identified this nonlinearity, possibly due to the relative lack of data information in datasets with few failures. The data set used here is unusually rich, in two senses: First, survival is measured on a monthly scale, which helps identify more precisely the moment of failure of financial institutions. Most of the previous studies use quarterly data, which is the frequency in which financial institutions report their balances to the supervisors in many countries. Second, due to Colombia's financial crisis, there are enough failures to identify and measure significant effects of financial variables. We expect that our qualitative results are likely to be applicable to modern banking systems generally, though we would hesitate to extrapolate numerical values of coefficients outside of our application.

Regarding the literature on the financial crisis of Colombia, this paper contributes by providing microeconomic evidence on the main variables determining bank failure. It also provides a model that can be used as an early warning tool and an alternative to the costly on-site visits made by supervisors to institutions considered at risk. It also provides the supervisors a basic guideline about which financial variables are important to follow during moments of stress.

Section 2 briefly describes what happened during the episode of financial crisis in Colombia. Section 3 presents the description of the data. Section 4 presents the techniques used to construct a model for the failure of financial institutions. Section 5 presents the results of the estimation as well as empirical tests to check the validity of the model. Section 6 presents some empirical evidence using time-varying regressors. Finally, section 7 presents conclusions.

2 The financial crisis in Colombia

During the 1980s, Colombia's financial system was subject to elevated reserve requirements and forced investments and to strong constraints on foreign investment. There were as well on the types of operations that intermediaries could do and on interest rates[2]. Additionally, a process of bank nationalization was held during that decade. In contrast, at the beginning of the 1990s, a program of financial liberalization was implemented. The process was supported by the laws 45 of 1990 and 9 of 1991, which eased the conditions for the entrance of foreign investment to Colombia, promoted more competition in the financial system, and gave financial institutions more liberty in the management of financial operations and interest rates (Banxo de la República, 2002).

As a result, the ratio of intermediated assets (loans plus bonds) to GDP increased from 31 percent in 1990 to 47 percent in 1996. The number of financial institutions increased significantly, the participation of the assets of foreign banks in the total assets of the system increased, and most of the government-owned financial institutions were privatized.

As a consequence of the growth in the financial system and of the economic expansion that took place during the first half of the 1990s, between 1991 and 1997 Colombia registered a credit boom without precedent. The ratio of loans to GDP and the price of assets (financial and real) grew steadily, as did the number of intermediaries. But, as is often the case when quick expansion of credit follows financial liberalization[3], the quality of loans of financial institutions decreased, and this degradation of loan quality elevated the financial fragility of the economy[4]. Between 1998 and 1999 a sudden capital reversion occurred, followed by a steep fall in the terms of trade, which led to a reduction in the aggregate level of expenditure. This has been identified as the main cause of both the financial crisis

---

[2] These were requirements imposed by the *Superintendencia Bancaria*, which at the time of the crisis was the regulator of the financial system in Colombia.

[3] For example, Carree (2003) argues that the process of bank liquidation that occurred in Russia during the period 1995-1998 (the Central Bank of Russia withdrew about 1000 bank licenses during that period) can be explained by the period of easing in financial regulation policies that took place during the early 1990s.

[4] During the ascendant part of the cycle, the fragilities of the financial system were not very visible. Most of the financial intermediaries obtained high profitability levels that arose from the higher levels of risk undertaken by them, as well as by low levels of provisions. When the downturn began, financial fragility became evident as loans deteriorated, deteriorating the financial systems' capital.

and the economic recession experienced in Colombia recently (Villar et al ,2005). Internal demand fell, especially during 1999, as well as output, while interest rates increased to historically high levels. However, as Parra and Salazar (2000) argue, monetary policy also played a role in increasing the vulnerability of the system, when in June 1998, the Central Bank while defending the exchange rate band added extra pressure on interest rates. The average interest rate on ninety-day *Certificados de Deposito a Termino* (CDT's)[5] increased more that 500 basis points in one month, while the average interest rate on loans increased almost 1000 basis points in the same period of time. From that moment on, a sharp deterioration of the financial health of the intermediaries began. Loan quality decreased - i.e., the rate of non-performing loans to total loans for the system increased from 7.9% in June 1998 to 16% by the end of 1999-, and the losses of financial institutions, which had very low levels of provisions, led to a reduction of capital and a worsening of capitalization. The reduction in the capitalization ratio was common for all the institutions but was asymmetric, doing more damage to those that had low capitalization levels before the crisis. Most of those institutions were liquidated, either forced by the Superintendencia Bancaria (hereafter Superbancaria, the financial system's supervisor) or voluntarily. Others merged, or were absorbed by other financial institutions.

The liquidation process of financial institutions is regulated by the *Estatuto Orgánico del Sistema Financiero* (Suberbancaria, 2006). The decision to liquidate an institution is taken to protect the depositors and the financial stability of the system. When a decision to liquidate is taken by the Superbancaria, it becomes effective immediately. The legal representative of the institution and the general public are informed about the decision and the Superbancaria takes control of the institution. The Superbancaria then chooses a liquidator who is in charge of liquidating the assets of the bank and repaying the depositors and other creditors of the failed institution.

The period of financial stress generated a reduction in the size of the financial intermediation industry of Colombia and a change in the asset composition of the financial system. In terms of size, the ratio of intermediated assets to GDP fell to 38 percent in 2000. In terms of asset composition, the percentage of loans in the assets of banks fell; in their place, more securities were acquired. Financial institutions became more conservative in their lending policies, in order to maintain

---

[5] Mainly time deposits issued by financial institutions to finance their positions in assets.

higher capitalization levels. Similarly, the ratio of provisions to loans of surviving institutions grew steadily. As a consequence, concentration of the financial system increased, mainly due to the processes of liquidation and mergers and acquisitions of institutions that took place during the period of stress.

3   Description of the data

In June 1998 there were 110 institutions in the financial system of Colombia, excluding financial cooperatives and special public financial institutions. From those institutions considered here as the financial system, 39 were commercial banks, 43 were financial companies, and the remaining 28 were financial companies specialized in commercial leasing. Three and a half years later, the financial system comprised only 57 institutions: 27 commercial banks, 19 financial companies, and 11 financial companies specializing in commercial leasing.

Although there are some differences between commercial banks and financial companies, due to liability composition[6] and size, in practical terms both types of institutions serve very similar purposes and compete in the issuance of loans and deposits. However, financial companies that specialize in commercial leasing are quite different, because they have different purposes than the other intermediaries previously mentioned, and their activities and portfolio composition are also very different. Therefore, for the purpose of this paper, data are collected only from commercial banks and financial companies.

Since we are interested in explaining time to failure during the financial crisis, the period of observation is the 42 months between June 1998, when the crisis began, and December 2001, when the system began to recover. Financial data as of June 1998 was collected for each of the financial institutions considered for the empirical analysis[7]. Following previous studies and theoretical expectations, the following financial ratios were considered in the explanation of time to failure: capitalization (CAP), defined as the ratio of equity to assets; management efficiency

---

[6]The main difference can be found in demand deposits: while commercial banks can issue checking accounts, financial companies cannot. Nevertheless, financial companies can issue saving deposits and time deposits. Another difference is the required amount of initial capital: the minimum required capital to constitute a bank is almost three times as big as that needed to constitute a financial company. Nevertheless, initial capital requirements are small vis-à-vis the size of the intermediaries once they are operating.

[7]For an extension reported in Section 6, we collect monthly data on each of the financial variables.

(EFF), approximated by the ratio of operating expenses to average annual assets; profitability of assets (PROF), given by the ratio of annualized profits to average annual assets; loan participation (LOAN), given by total loans over total assets; loan composition (COMP), defined as the ratio of commercial loans to total loans; and, a market based variable (SIZE), defined as the assets of the institution divided by a common number to scale the variable appropriately. These financial indicators are proxies of the variables traditionally considered in the literature. The variables COMP and LOAN can be interpreted as portfolio characteristics potentially related to volatility.

This paper emphasizes the special role played by the capitalization ratio, identifying a non-linear impact of this ratio on time to bank failure in Colombia. To account for a non-linear component of capitalization, a variable called CAPL was included. This variable results from the multiplication of (CAP-C) by an indicator function that takes the value 1 if CAP is less or equal to C and 0 otherwise. We experimented with different values of C. Our purpose here is to approximate a nonlinearity of unknown functional form with a simple approximation. As it turns out, the data are informative enough to identify a significant nonlinearity, but not informative enough to tie down its functional form precisely.

The data set used to construct the variables consists of information in the balance sheets that financial institutions have to report to the Superbancaria. Table 1 shows a summary of the indicators for both groups of intermediaries in June 1998.

Table 1: Summary of the financial ratios used in the empirical analysis
(In percentage for all variables, except SIZE, measured in millions of Colombian pesos)

Banks	Percentile			Others	Percentile			Overall	Percentile		
	25	50	75		25	50	75		25	50	75
CAP	8.7	12.8	15.4	CAP	13.3	18.1	29.0	CAP	11.4	14.4	21.0
EFF	3.1	3.9	5.1	EFF	1.5	2.5	3.6	EFF	2.3	3.3	4.4
PROF	-0.3	0.6	0.9	PROF	-1.2	0.08	0.9	PROF	-0.7	0.3	0.9
LOAN	58.4	66.3	77.5	LOAN	58.5	67.5	73.2	LOAN	58.5	67.3	75.2
COMP	26.7	70.2	81.1	COMP	23.1	63.3	99.4	COMP	24.9	67.5	91.0
SIZE	432.2	980.1	2452.8	SIZE	36.4	110.1	275.5	SIZE	103.2	299.9	1196

Looking at medians, financial companies appear to be more capitalized than banks, and to be smaller, more efficient and less profitable also. However, there are large variations within each type of institution. Note also that medians of asset and loan composition are similar for banks and financial companies; in this sense, the latter can be considered as small banks. Most correlations between the variables were small and in no case did one exceed 0.51 in absolute value.

Regarding failure, from the group of banks 12 failures were observed between June 1998 and December 2001, representing a failure rate of 31 percent; meanwhile, 16 institutions of the group of non-banks failed during the same period, representing a failure rate of 37 percent[8]. Overall, there are 82 institutions in the sample, of which 28 failed. Failure rates of both groups of intermediaries appear similar. In the next section tests are done to show that both groups have the same survivor function.

4 Duration models to study bank failure

We use a duration or hazard function model to study the time to failure of financial institutions. This approach generalizes the more common binary response (logit or probit) approach by modeling not only the occurrence of failure but the time to failure - allowing finer measurement of the effect of different variables on failure. Thus, duration models applied to this problem can provide answers to questions that are relevant for both financial supervisors and financial institutions, such as: after the occurrence of a negative shock, what is the probability that a bank fails in the following months, given it has survived up to that moment? Or, what is the predicted time to failure for a bank of some given characteristics? A model capable of answering those questions at low cost can be very useful as an early warning model, to identify potential vulnerabilities of the financial system, and could be used by supervisors as an alternative to the costly site visits that they make periodically to financial institutions considered at risk.

---

[8] In this paper, failure is considered as the event in which an institution is liquidated, either by the decision of the regulator (forced failure) or by the decision of the institution's managers ("voluntary" failure). The moment in which the bank fails is defined as the month in which the institution is liquidated formally; that is, the moment at which the institution stops reporting its balances to the Superbancaria. Even when this is not a exact measure of the moment in which a bank fails, it appears to be the best possible approximation, and the fact that the balance sheets of financial institutions are reported on a monthly frequency, rather than a quarterly frequency as in other countries makes this measure more accurate. Institutions that merged or were acquired are not considered as a failure here.

Most of the papers that apply these models to explain time to bank failure use the semiparametric proportional hazards model of Cox (1972); an exception is the work of Carree (2003), who uses several parametric models to explain bank failure in Russia. The proportional hazards model is the most frequently used, because it does not make assumptions about the particular functional form of the baseline hazard, and because estimated hazard functions of bank failure in many cases are non-monotonic, thus reducing the number of parametric models that can be used.

4.1   Survivor functions and hazard functions

In duration models, the dependent variable is duration, the time that takes a system to change from one state to another. In the case of bank failure, duration is the time that it takes for a bank to fail after the occurrence of a negative shock that affects the financial system.

In theory, duration T is a non-negative, continuous random variable. However, in practice, duration is usually represented by an integer number of months, for example. When T can take a large number of integer values, it is conventional to model duration as being continuous (Davidson and MacKinnon, 2004).

Duration can be represented by its density function $f(t)$ or its cumulative distribution function $F(t)$, where $F(t) = Pr(T \leq t)$, for a given t. The survival function, which is an alternative way of representing duration, is given by $S(t) = 1 - F(t) = Pr(T > t)$. In words, the survival function represents the probability that the duration of an event is larger than a given t. Now, the probability that a state ends between period t and $t + \Delta t$, given that it has lasted up to time t, is given by

$$Pr(t < T \leq t + \Delta t \mid T > t) = \frac{F(t + \Delta t) - F(t)}{S(t)} \tag{1}$$

This is the conditional probability that the state ends in a short time after t, provided it has reached time t. For example, in the case of bank failure it is the probability that a bank changes of state from operating to not operating (i.e. fails) in a short time after time t, conditional on the fact that the bank was still operating at time t.

The hazard function $\lambda(t)$, which is another way of characterizing the distribution of T, results from considering the limit when $\Delta t \to 0$ of equation (1). This function gives the instantaneous probability rate that a change of state occurs, given that it has not happened up to moment t. The cumulative hazard function $\Lambda(t)$ is the integral of the hazard function. The relation between the hazard function, the cumulative hazard function and the survival function is given by equation (2)

$$\Lambda(t) = \int\limits_{u=0}^{t} \lambda(u)du = -\log[S(t)] \tag{2}$$

Some empirical studies use parametric models for duration. Commonly used distributions are the exponential, the Weibull and the Gompertz. The exponential implies a constant hazard while the Weibull admits decreasing or increasing hazards. The Gompertz distribution allows non-monotonic hazard rates, but is not particularly flexible. Further, the baseline hazard in our formulation reflects changes in macroeconomic conditions common to all the institutions. There is no reason to think these will correspond to a monotonic hazard, and indeed we find evidence it does not.

We begin by estimating the unconditional (raw: no covariates) survivor function, using the Kaplan-Meier non-parametric estimator, which takes into account censored data. Suppose that bank failure is observed at different moments in time, $t_1, t_2, ..., t_m$, and that d_i banks fail at time t_i[9] For $t \geq t_i$,

$$\hat{S}(t) = \prod_{t_i \leq t} \left[1 - \frac{d_i}{N_i} \right] \tag{3}$$

where N_i represents the total number of banks that were still operating at time t_i. The failure pattern of banks and of other financial institutions during the financial crisis of Colombia was similar in terms of percentage of institutions failing. That suggests that the survival functions of both groups might be similar. Table 2 shows summary data about the dynamics of financial institutions failure. Figure 1 shows the estimated survival function for both groups of intermediaries. These look similar. In order to corroborate that intuition, tests of equality of the survival functions were done. Table 3 shows the results of these tests. Note that these tests are crude and exploratory because they do not condition on the bank-specific financial variables. Nevertheless, they give us some confidence that pooling is appropriate, because, as can be observed from Table 3, there is no evidence to reject the null hypothesis of equality of the survival functions of both groups. Therefore, in the rest of the paper we treat all the institutions as one group. The Kaplan-Meier survival function for the whole group of institutions is shown in

---

[9]Note that in continuous time there should be no ties in time of failure among banks. Nevertheless, in practice ties are observed.

Figure 2.

Table 3: Test for equality of the survivor functions

Ho : Both groups have equal survival functions

$Test$	$\chi^2(1)$	$Prob > \chi^2$
$Log-rank$	0.45	0.5039
$Wicoxon$	0.41	0.5238

In order to estimate the hazard function, it is first required to obtain an estimation of the cumulative hazard function. The Nelson-Aalen non-parametric estimator is natural for this purpose. Equation (4) shows how to compute this estimator. For $t \geq t_i$

$$\hat{\Lambda}(t) = \sum_{t_i \leq t} \frac{d_i}{N_i} \tag{4}$$

The hazard function can be estimated as a kernel-smoothed representation of the estimated hazard contributions[10] $\Delta \hat{\Lambda}(t_i) = \hat{\Lambda}(t_i) - \hat{\Lambda}(t_{i-1})$, as

$$\hat{\lambda}(t) = \frac{1}{b} \sum_{i=1}^{D} K\left(\frac{t-t_i}{b}\right) \Delta \hat{\Lambda}(t_i) \tag{5}$$

where $K()$ represents the kernel function, b is the bandwidth, and the summation is over the total number of failures D that is observed (Klein and Moeschberger, 2003).

Figure 3 shows the estimated smoothed-hazard function for the group of financial institutions. Note how the hazard rate of failure is clearly non-monotonic. Initially it increases sharply up to approximately month 10, then decreases up to month 25, then increases a little and finally decreases from month 30 on. This behavior of the baseline hazard reflects events applying to all institutions, like changes in macroeconomic conditions during the time of the study. Of particular importance, there was a change in the exchange rate regime in September 1999, from a crawling-peg system to a free-floating system.

The form of the estimated hazard function shows that the most commonly used

---

[10]The kernel-smoothed estimator of $\lambda(t)$ is a weighted average of these "crude" estimates over event times close to t. How close the events are is determined by b, the bandwidth, so that events lying in the interval [t-b, t+b] are included in the weighted average. The kernel function determines the weights given to points at a distance from t. Here we use the Epanechnikov kernel.

parametric models for the distribution of duration do not seem to be appropriate for modeling the baseline hazard of bank failure in Colombia during the period of financial stress.

4.2 Proportional hazards

Our objective is to understand how bank-specific variables affected the conditional probability of failure and time to failure after the shocks that initiated the financial crisis. In ordinary regression models, explanatory variables affect the dependent variable by moving its mean around. However, in duration models it is not straightforward to see how explanatory variables affect duration and the interpretation of the coefficients in these types of models depends on the particular specification of the model. But there are two widely used special cases in which the coefficients can be given a partial derivative interpretation: the proportional hazards model and the accelerated lifetime model (Kiefer, 1988).

Following the previous literature on the application of duration models to bank failure and building on the above analysis indicating that conventional candidates for parametric models are inappropriate, this paper estimates a proportional hazards model in which no parametric form is assumed for the baseline hazard function. As shown below using a specification test, this assumption seems to be appropriate for the problem of interest.

Under the proportional hazards specification the hazard rate can be written as

$$\lambda(t, x, \beta, \lambda_0) = \phi(x, \beta)\lambda_0(t) \tag{6}$$

where λ_0 is the baseline hazard. Note that the effect of time on the hazard rate is captured completely through the baseline hazard. One common specification for the function ϕ, which is followed in this paper, is $\phi(x, \beta) = \exp(x'\beta)$, where x is a vector of covariates and β is the corresponding vector of parameters to be estimated. Under this specification

$$\frac{\partial \log[\lambda(\cdot)]}{\partial x_k} = \beta_k \tag{7}$$

for all k. Therefore, the coefficients can be interpreted as the constant, proportional effect of the corresponding covariate on the conditional probability of completing a spell. In the particular case of bank failure, completing a spell is associ-

11

ated with the moment in which a bank is liquidated.

4.3 Estimation technique

In the case of specifications which model the baseline hazard explicitly by making use of a particular parametric model, estimation can be done by the method of maximum likelihood. When the baseline hazard is not explicitly modeled, the conventional estimation method is partial likelihood estimation, developed by Cox (1972). The key point of the method is the observation that the ratio of the hazards (6) for any two individuals i and j depends on the covariates, but does not depend on duration:

$$\frac{\lambda(t, x_i, \beta, \lambda_0)}{\lambda(t, x_j, \beta, \lambda_0)} = \frac{\exp(x_i'\beta)}{\exp(x_j'\beta)} \tag{8}$$

Suppose there are n observations and there is no censoring. If there are no ties, durations can be ordered from the shortest to the longest, $t_1 < t_2 < ... < t_n$. Note that the index denotes both the observation and the moment of time in which the duration for that particular observation ends. The contribution to the partial likelihood function of any observation j is given by

$$\frac{\exp(x_j'\beta)}{\sum_{i=j}^{n} \exp(x_i'\beta)} \tag{9}$$

the ratio of the hazard of the individual whose spell ended at duration t_j to the sum of the hazards of the individual whose spells were still in progress at the instant before t_j. The likelihood can then be written as

$$L(\beta) = \prod_{j=1}^{n} \frac{\exp(x_j'\beta)}{\sum_{i=j}^{n} \exp(x_i'\beta)} \tag{10}$$

Thus, the log-likelihood function is

$$\ell(\beta) = \sum_{j=1}^{n} \left[x_j'\beta - \log \sum_{i=j}^{n} \exp(x_j'\beta) \right] \tag{11}$$

By maximizing equation (11) with respect to β, estimators of the unknown parameter values are obtained. The intuition behind partial likelihood estimation is that without knowing the baseline hazard only the order of durations provides information about the unknown coefficients.

When there is censoring, the censored spells will contribute to the log-likelihood function by entering only in the denominator of the uncensored observations. Censored observations will not enter the numerator of the log-likelihood function at all.

Ties in durations can be handled by several different methods. In this paper, ties are handled by applying the Breslow method. In continuous time ties are not expected. Nevertheless, given that the moment of failure in practical applications is aggregated into groups (here months), ties are possible, and in fact they occur. Suppose we have 4 individuals a_1, a_2, a_3, a_4, in the risk pool and in a certain moment a_1 and a_2 fail. The Breslow method says that, given it is unknown which of the failures preceded the other, the largest risk pool will be used for both failures. In other words, this method assumes that a_1 failed from the risk pool a_1, a_2, a_3, a_4, and a_2 also failed from the risk pool a_1, a_2, a_3, a_4. The Breslow method is an approximation of the exact marginal likelihood, and is used when there are not many ties at a given point in time.

5 Estimation results

The model was estimated using the partial likelihood method. Results are presented in Table 4, which shows the values of the estimated coefficients and their standard errors. One first important conclusion from Table 4 is that the null hypothesis that none of the indicators included in the model is important in explaining the behavior of duration is clearly rejected. This provides evidence that supports the idea that failure of financial institutions during the period of financial stress can be explained by differences in financial health and prudence existing across institutions. Given our focus on capitalization and the differences observed in the median values of this ratio for banks and financial companies, we included a slope dummy (DCAP) to test whether the effect of this variable on the hazard rate differs between the two types of institutions. The "t" statistic, for the test of the hypothesis that the effect of this interaction variable is zero, is 0.21. This is not a surprising value under the null; the probability under the null of seeing this or a higher value is 0.83. Thus, we focus discussion on the constrained estimates in the last 2 columns of Table 4.

Regarding the role played by individual indicators, it can be seen that the single most significant financial ratio in explaining the inter-institution variability in the hazard rate is the capitalization ratio. The sign of the coefficient is negative, implying that an increase in the capitalization ratio for a given bank results in a reduction of its probability of failing at every moment of time, everything else constant. This is the expected result, consistent with previous studies and verifying the importance to both the institutions and their supervisors of following the evolution of this ratio over time. More important and novel is the finding that the variable CAPL affects the hazard rate significantly and with the expected negative sign[11]. This provides evidence in favor of a non-linear effect of the capitalization ratio on the probability of failure. Therefore, improvements in this ratio are more important for poorly capitalized banks than for banks with better capitalization levels. This result can be explained intuitively. It can be expected that there is a capitalization level over which a bank no longer benefits from a further increase, and, on the contrary, could loose profitable lending opportunities. The estimated coefficients for CAP and CAPL imply that a one percentage point increase in the capitalization ratio will lead to a 6.0 percent reduction of the instantaneous probability of failure for a well-capitalized bank (capitalization greater than C; for these specific numbers C=10.2%. Very similar results hold for a range of values of C), while it will lead to a 25.3 percent reduction in the same probability for a poorly capitalized bank (capitalization less than C), everything else being constant. Note that this direct interpretation of the coefficient compares a percentage point change with a percentage change. Given these coefficient estimates, a one percent increase in capitalization from the cutoff value of 10.2 percent will reduce the sample average per period failure rate from 0.81 percent to 0.76 percent, while a one percent decrease in capitalization will increase the rate to 1.02%[12].

---

[11] Table 4 reports the results setting the value of C equal to 10.2 percent. Nevertheless, these results remain valid for values of C in the range from 10 to 11 percent.

[12] A one percent change in the capitalization ratio is rather large and is not frequently observed in a short period for a financial institution. Therefore, the numerical interpretation of the coefficients here should be considered as a reference only.

Table 4: Partial likelihood estimation results

	Unconstrained model		Constrained model	
Variable	Coefficient	Std. Err.	Coefficient	Std. Err.
CAP	-.0595	.0302	-.0596	.0302
CAPL	-.2057	.1141	-.1933	.0975
EFF	-.1684	.2096	-.1434	.1738
PROF	-.1696	.1256	-.1572	.1108
LOAN	-.0128	.0151	-.0128	.0152
COMP	.0067	.0097	.0078	.0083
SIZE	-.0011	.0005	-.0011	.0005
DCAP	.0077	.0366		
Log-likelihood	-97.81		-97.83	
LR $\chi^2(d.f.)$	25.45 (8)		25.41 (7)	
Prob$>\chi^2$	.0013		.0006	

Another important variable in explaining the hazard rate is bank's size (SIZE). The sign is negative, indicating that, other things being equal, increases in this variable decrease the risk of failure of a bank. This effect is the expected one, as it seems reasonable to assume that large institutions are less exposed to risk because they can diversify their assets more, because they can achieve economies of scale, or because they likely have been in business longer. Profitability (PROF) is also important and its coefficient is negative, as expected, although its significance is lower.

As a robustness test for the results shown above, changes to the specification of the model were done by excluding variables and by including new ones. In all the different specifications, the signs of CAP and CAPL remained unchanged, and the values of the coefficients were stable. The same holds for regressions done exlcuding outlyers with very high and low capitalization levels.

The interpretation of the results presented in Table 4 relies on the proportional hazards assumption. Therefore, it is important to test whether this assumption is a sensible one in the context studied here. This can be done formally using the Schoenfeld's residuals test. The proportional hazards factorization implies that the effect of the covariates on the hazard function is constant over time. Testing the hypothesis that the effects of the covariates do not vary over time is equivalent to testing for a zero slope in a generalized linear regression of the residuals on time. The null hypothesis of the test is that the slope is zero. A rejection of the null hypothesis indicates that the proportional hazards assumption is unsuitable. It is a conventional practice to do a test of each covariate as well as a global test. Most absolute "t"'s were small, and the joint test statistic, a $\chi^2(7)$ random variable, takes the value 9.53, not a surprising value under the null that all the coefficients are zero. This provides evidence that the proportional hazards assumption is adequate in the context of the model of bank failure.

Figure 4 shows the estimated survival function evaluated at the mean values of all the predictors. Of course, this lines up well with the raw survivor function plotted in Figure 2. Figure 5 shows the estimated hazard functions evaluated with the value of capital one percentage point below the break value, at the break value, and one percentage point above. The other predictors are held constant at their means. Figure 5 gives striking summary evidence on the importance of capitalization on the likelihood of default in a period of financial stress.

6   Time varying regressors

The model estimated in the previous section is useful for banks and supervisors, because the probability that a bank fails in a certain future period can be calculated using only financial data on the bank that is currently available. Tests of the proportional hazards assumption showed that the specification considered previously is adequate. As a further description of the failure process, from a somewhat different point of view, we consider a regression model with time varying covariates. The specification is retained, but now monthly observations on each regressor from June 1998 to December 2001 are used.

Table 5 shows the results of the regression done by partial likelihood estimation, using time varying covariates. The signs of the coefficients of the variables remain unchanged. Some changes are observed regarding the significance levels of the variables. Particularly, the significance of capitalization is reduced, while profitability gains significance. The chi-squared statistic, twice the difference in log-likelihood values, for the test of the joint hypothesis that the effect of CAP and CAPL is zero, is 3.78. On two degrees of freedom, the probability under the null of seeing this or a higher value is 0.15.

When combined with the previous results, we conclude that, when considering a bank's viability into the future, current capitalization is the key financial variable. When considering immediate risk, current profitability is also important. Perhaps both variables are important indicators of financial health, but profitability is more idiosyncratic and has a more immediate effect, while capitalization is a less noisy indicator of financial health. Thus, profitability at a point in time reflects "shocks" specific to that period, while capitalization is less affected by single-period shocks. Profitability looses significance in the longer run, probably because current profitability is not a good forecast of future profitability, while capitalization, affected by accumulated profits, is less temporally variable.

Table 5: Time varying regressors

	Unconstrained model		Constrained model	
Variable	Coefficient	Std. Err.	Coefficient	Std. Err.
CAP	-.0045	.0149		
CAPL	-.0286	.0229		
EFF	-.0064	.0524	-.0006	.0516
PROF	-.0433	.02100	-.0686	.0147
LOAN	-.0222	.0126	-.0151	.0101
COMP	.0003	.0070	.0027	.0068
SIZE	-.0007	.0003	-.0009	.0004
Log-likelihood	-93.59		-95.48	
LR $\chi^2(d.f.)$	42.74 (7)		38.96 (5)	
Prob>χ^2	.0000		.0000	

7 Conclusions

This paper identifies the main bank-specific determinants of time to failure during the financial crisis in Colombia. Using an unusually informative data set and a duration model with partial likelihood estimation, we show that the process of failure of financial institutions during that period is significantly affected by differences in financial health and prudence existing across institutions. Our specification tests show that the proportional hazard specification is appropriate for our sample, while popular parametric specifications of the baseline hazard are unsatisfactory.

When looking ahead, the capitalization ratio is the most significant of the relevant indicators that explain bank failure. Increases in this ratio lead to a reduction in the hazard rate of failure at any given moment in time. This ratio exhibits a non-linear component, implying that the impact of increases in this variable is more important for less capitalized banks. This result, which appears to be intuitive and appealing, agrees with the literature on capital crunch that suggests that banks' capital is crucial for real decisions taken by banks, such as portfolio choices. Related previous studies have found capitalization to be a significant variable explaining the conditional probability of failure; however, none identifies a nonlinear component. Other important variables explaining bank failure dynamics are a bank's size and profitability.

When using time-varying covariates, profitability gains significance as a short-run indicator of instantaneous failure. This result indicates that profitability is an important indicator of within-period feasibility of the bank, while capitalization is a less noisy indicator of financial health.

References

Arias, A.; A. Carrasquilla, and A. Galindo (1999): "Credit Crunch: a Liquidity Channel", Mimeo Banco de la República.

Arbeláez, M.A., and S. Zuluaga (2002): "Impuestos Implícitos y Explícitos al Sector Financiero Colombiano: 1995-2001", in El Sector Financiero de Cara al Siglo XXI ANIF(eds.), 257-344.

Banco de la República (2002): *Financial Stability Report*.

Basel Committee on Banking Supervision (2004): International Convergence of Capital Measurement and Capital Standards: A Revised Framework, Bank for International Settlements.

Carrasquilla, A., and J.P. Zárate (2002): "Regulación Bancaria y Tensión Financiera: 1998-2001", in El Sector Financiero de Cara al Siglo XXI ANIF(eds.), 215-230.

Carree, M.A. (2003): "A Hazard Rate Analysis of Russian Commercial Banks in the Period 1994-1997", Economic Systems, 27, 255-269.

Cox, D.R. (1972): "Regression Models and Life-Tables", Journal of the Royal Statistical Society, B 34, 187-220.

Davidson, R., and J.G. MacKinnon (2004): <u>Econometric Theory and Methods</u>, Oxford University Press, Chapter 11.

Estrella, A.; S. Park, and S. Peristiani (2000). "Capital ratios as predictors of bank failure," <u>Economic Policy Review</u>, 6, 33-52.

Gonzalez-Hermosillo, B.; C. Pazarbasioglu, and R. Billings (1996): "Banking System Fragility: Likelihood Versus Timing of Failure: an Application to the Mexican Financial Crisis", IMF Working Paper.

Kiefer, N.M. (1988): "Economic Duration Data and Hazard Functions", <u>Journal of Economic Literature</u>, XXVI, 646-679.

Klein, J.P., and M.L. Moeschberger (2003): Survival Analysis. Techniques for Censored and Truncated Data, Second Edition, Springer.

Lancaster, T. (1990): "The Econometric Analysis of Transition Data", <u>Econometric Society Monographs</u>, 17, Cambridge University Press.

Lane, W.R.; S. Looney and J. Wansley (1986): "An Application of the Cox Proportional Hazards Model to Bank Failure", <u>Journal of Banking and Finance</u>, 10, 511-531.

Parra, C.E. and N. Salazar (2000). "La Crisis Financiera y la Experiencia Internacional", <u>Boletines de Divulgacion Economica DNP</u>, 1.

Peek, J., and E.S. Rosengren (1995). "Bank Regulation and the Credit Crunch", <u>Journal of Banking and Finance</u>, 19, 679-692.

Superintendencia Bancaria de Colombia (2006): *Estatuto Orgánico del Sistema Financiero*.

Uribe, J.D., and H. Vargas (2002): "Financial Reform, Crisis and Consolidation in Colombia", <u>Borradores de Economia Banrep</u>, 204.

Urrutia, M. (1999): "Credito y Reactivacion Economica", Editorial Note, <u>Revista del Banco de la Republica</u>, LXXII.

Villar, L.; D. Salamanca and A. Murcia (2005): "Credito, Represion Financiera y Flujos de Capitales en Colombia", <u>Borradores de Economia Banrep</u>, 322.

Van den Heuvel, S (2004): "The Bank Capital Channel of Monetary Policy", Mimeo, Wharton School University of Pennsylvania.

Weelock, D., and P. Wilson (1995): "Why Do Banks Disappear? The Determinants of U.S. Bank Failures and Acquisitions", Federal Reserve Bank of St. Louis, Working Paper No. 950133.

Whalen, G. (1991): "A Proportional Hazards Model of Bank Failure: An Examination of its Usefulness as an Early Warning Tool", Economic Review, 27, 21-30.

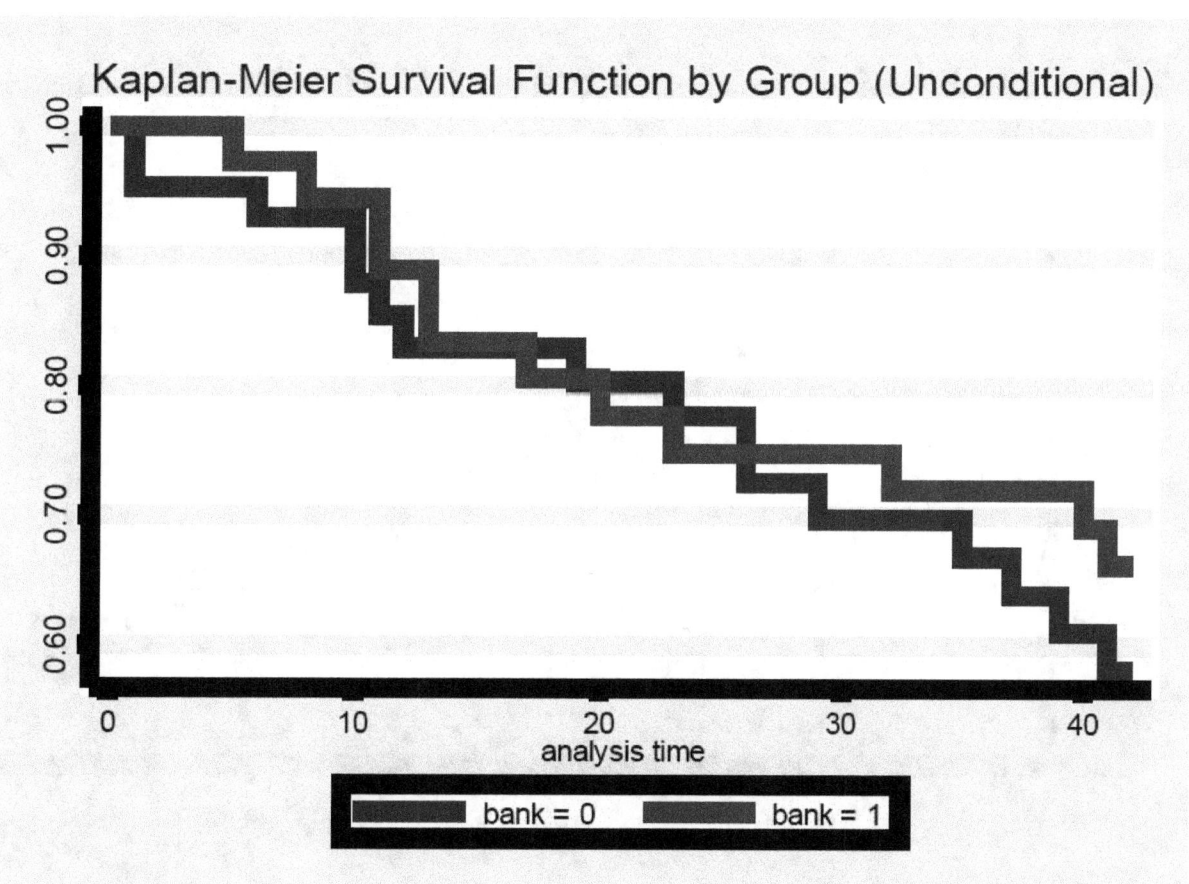

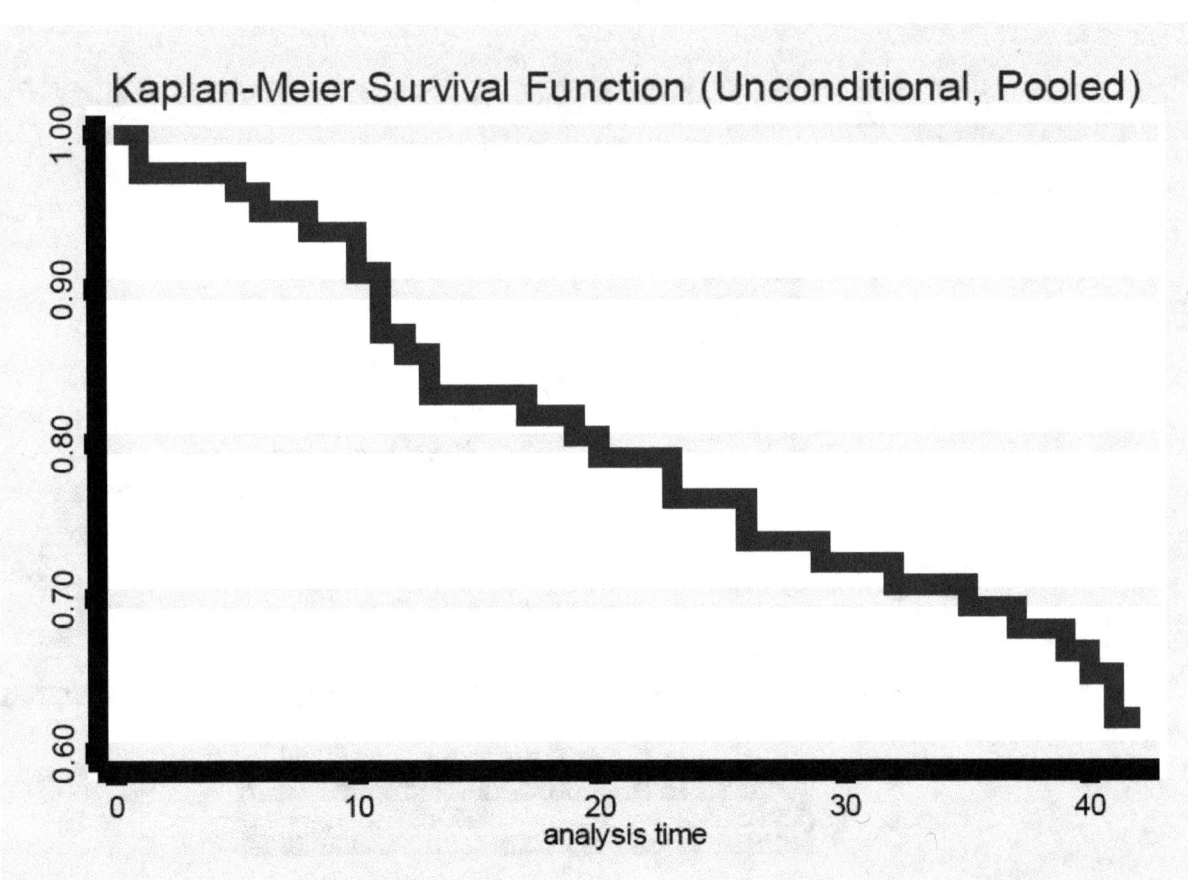

Kaplan-Meier Survival Function (Unconditional, Pooled)

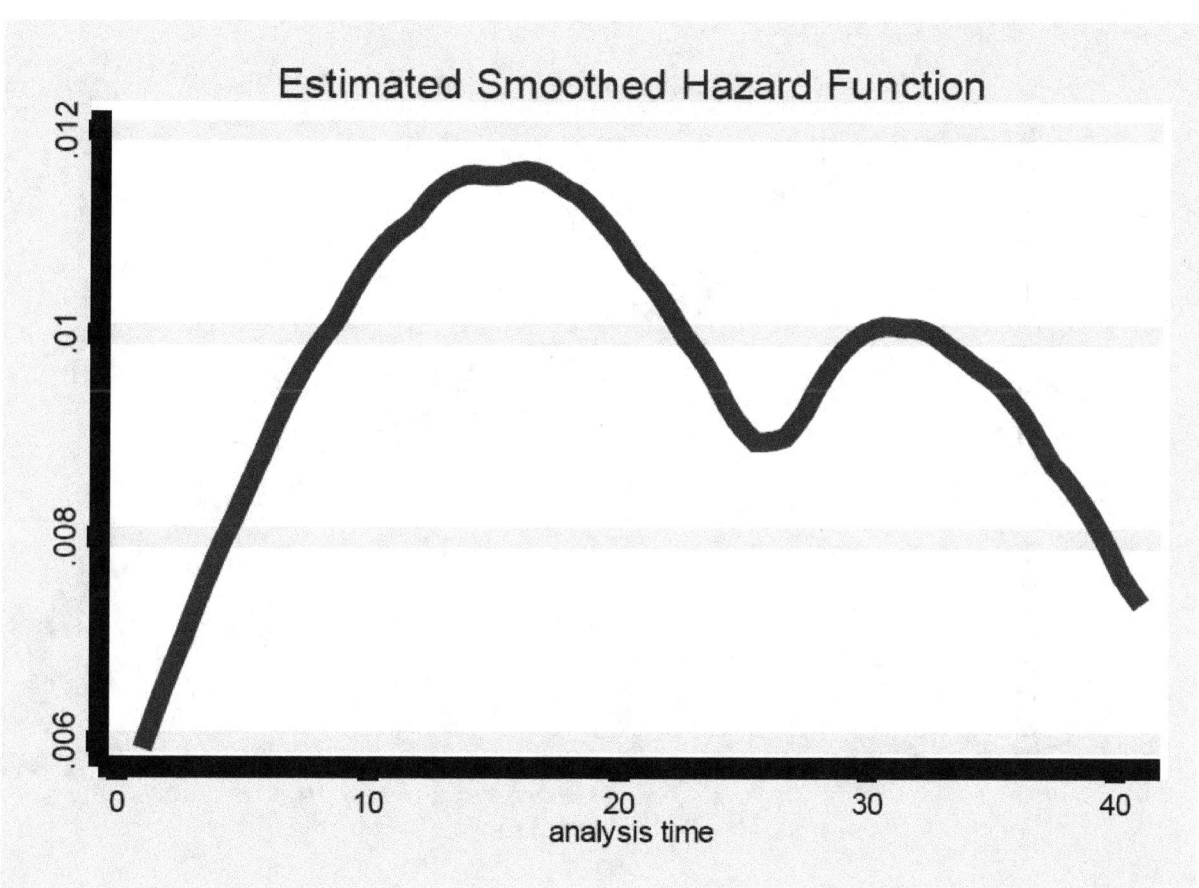

Estimated Smoothed Hazard Function

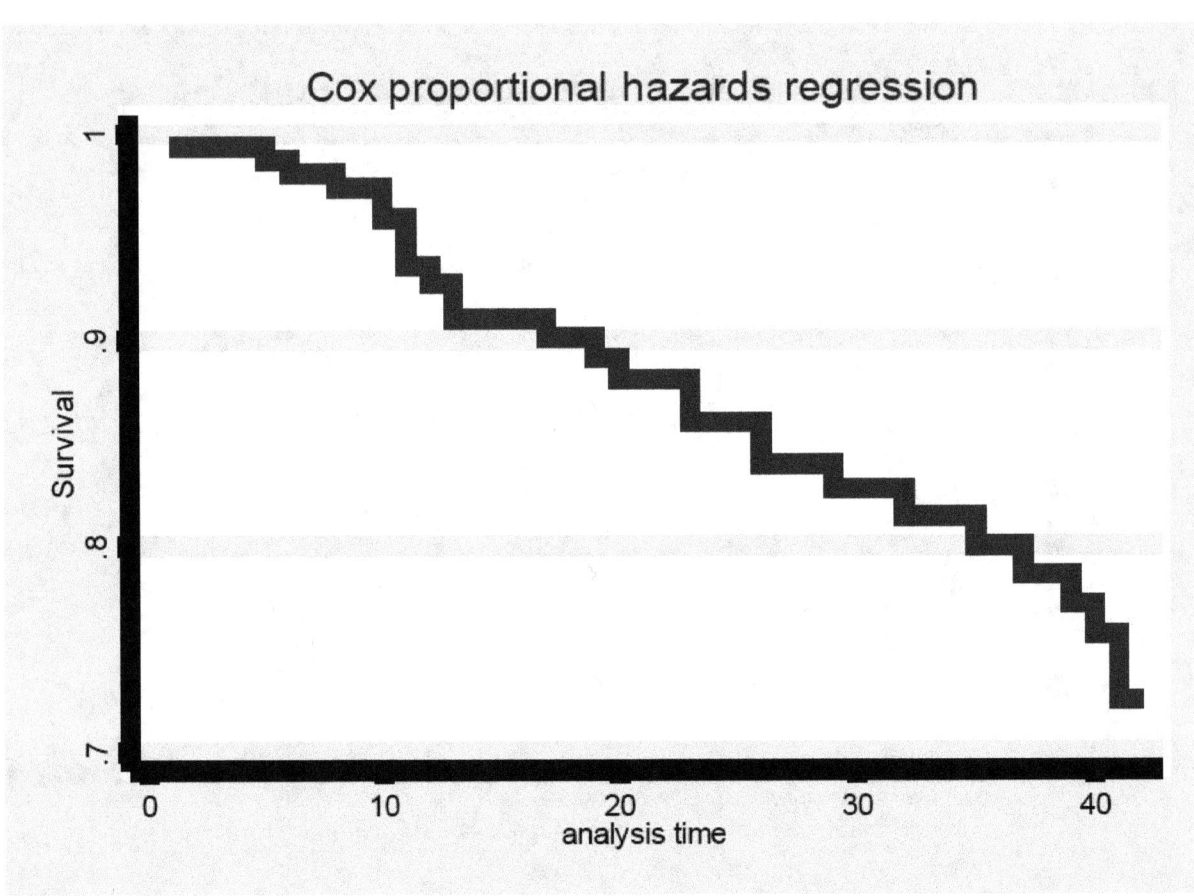

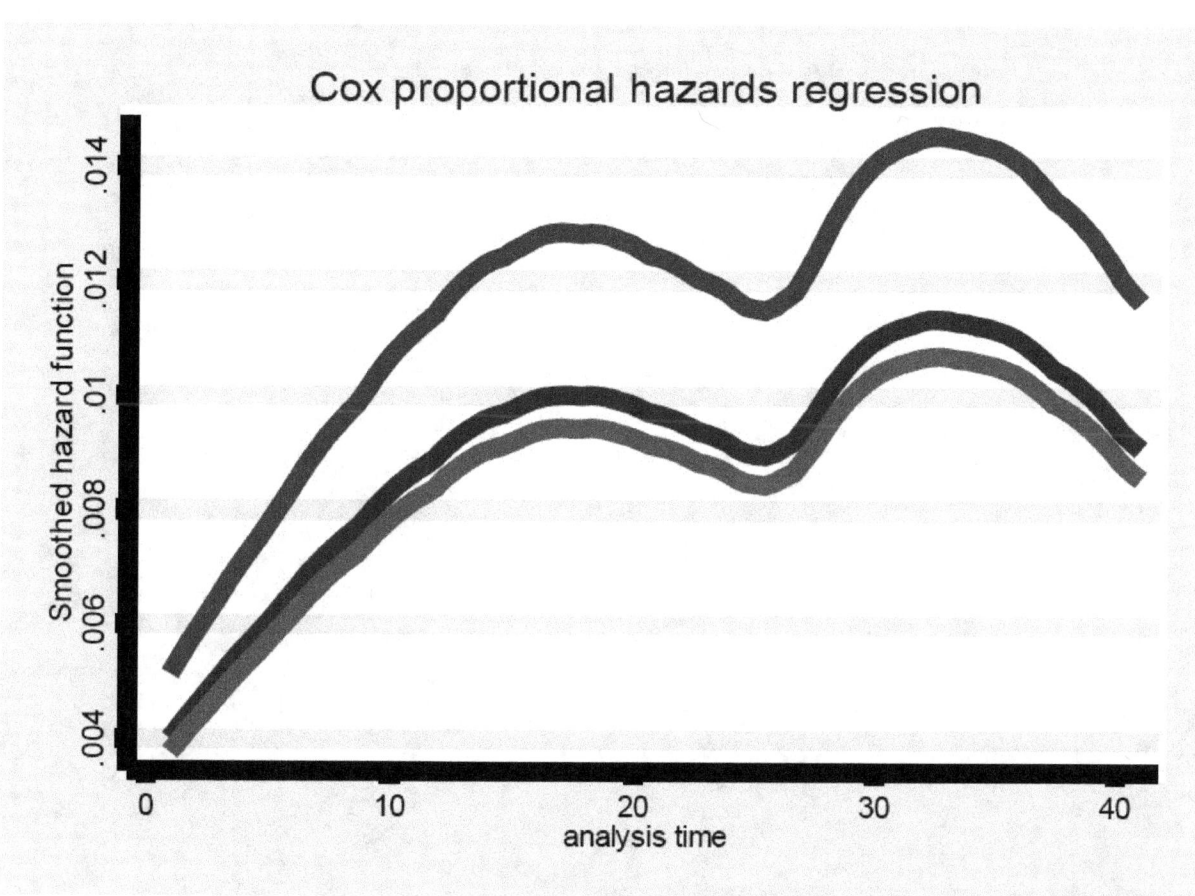

Figure 1: Top: CAP at 9.2%; Middle: CAP at 10.2%; Bottom: CAP at 11.2%